CENSORSHIP

What Is It and How Does It Impact Society?

Carla Mooney

ReferencePoint
Press

About the Author

Carla Mooney is the author of many books for young adults and children.
She lives in Pittsburgh, Pennsylvania, with her husband and three children.

For more information, contact:
ReferencePoint Press, Inc.
PO Box 27779
San Diego, CA 92198
www.ReferencePointPress.com

Picture Credits:

Cover: Marcos Mesa Sam Wordley/Shutterstock
    .com
 5: Brigette Supernova/Alamy Stock Photo
 9: Jacob Lund/Shutterstock.com
10: Heritage Image Partnership Ltd/Alamy Stock
    Photo
14: Associated Press
18: On the Run Photo/Shutterstock.com
20: Sueddeutsche Zeitung Photo/Alamy Stock
    Photo

24: Bob Daemmrich/ZUMAPRESS/Newscom
29: IanDagnall Computing/Alamy Stock Photo
32: Monkey Business Images/Shutterstock.com
34: The Old Major/Shutterstock.com
39: Rawpixel.com/Shutterstock.com
42: Ringo Chiu/Shutterstock.com
45: MediaPunch Inc/Alamy Stock Photo
48: John Nacion/Shutterstock.com
51: Kathy Hutchins/Shutterstock.com
55: ZUMA Press, Inc./Alamy Stock Photo

LIBRARY OF CONGRESS CATALOGING-IN-PUBLICATION DATA

Names: Mooney, Carla, author.
Title: Censorship : what is it and how does it impact society / by Carla Mooney.
Description: San Diego : ReferencePoint Press, 2024. | Includes
    bibliographical references and index.
Identifiers: LCCN 2023032243 (print) | LCCN 2023032244 (ebook) | ISBN
    9781678207267 (library binding) | ISBN 9781678207274 (ebook)
Subjects: LCSH: Censorship--United States--Juvenile literature. | Freedom
    of speech--United States--Juvenile literature. | Prohibited
    books--United States--Juvenile literature. | Social
    media--Censorship--Juvenile lIterature. | Cancel culture--United
    States--Juvenile literature.
Classification: LCC Z658.U5 M67 2024 (print) | LCC Z658.U5 (ebook) | DDC
    363.310973--dc23/eng/20230811
LC record available at https://lccn.loc.gov/2023032243
LC ebook record available at https://lccn.loc.gov/2023032244

Laws That Limit Expression

In March 2023 Lewis-Clark State College Center for Arts & History in Lewiston, Idaho, hosted an exhibition titled Unconditional Care: Listening to People's Health Needs. The college hired artist Katrina Majkut to curate the exhibit, which focused on health care issues, including chronic illness, pregnancy, and gun violence.

Majkut and two other artists were pulled aside a few days before the exhibit's opening. The artists were informed that some of their artwork was removed from the show because it included references to abortion. College administrators were worried that the artwork violated Idaho's No Public Funds for Abortion Act. The 2021 law barred state-funded entities, like the school, from using public money to promote abortion, provide abortions, or counsel someone to have an abortion.

A Shocking Removal

Majkut was shocked. She uses embroidery to create pieces highlighting historical ideas of being a wife and mother. One of her embroidery pieces portrayed two abortion medications that can trigger an abortion early in pregnancy. Before the Idaho show, her artwork had been shown without controversy in more than two dozen states over the previous ten years. Now her embroidery piece was removed from the Idaho exhibit. Other items removed included a wall plaque that listed Idaho's abortion laws, several documentary video and audio works that included women speaking about their abortion experiences, and a series of 1920s letters written to Planned Parenthood founder Margaret Sanger. "To be censored like that is shocking and surreal," says Majkut. "If the most even-keeled, bipartisan artwork around this topic is censored, then everything is going to be censored."[1]

A spokesperson for the college said that the school had consulted with attorneys about the exhibit and whether showing the art could violate the law. Together they decided to pull the artwork from the exhibition.

Free speech advocates condemned the college's actions. Scarlet Kim, a staff attorney with the American Civil Liberties Union (ACLU) Speech, Privacy, and Technology Project, said the organization has been monitoring how the Idaho law affects speech on public university campuses. Kim argues that it is concerning that

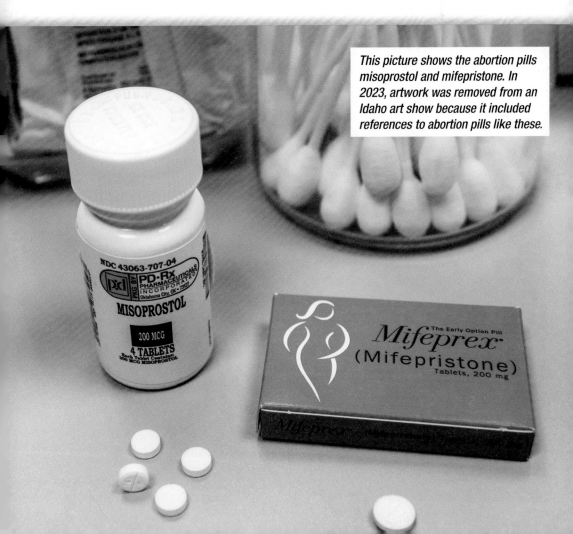

This picture shows the abortion pills misoprostol and mifepristone. In 2023, artwork was removed from an Idaho art show because it included references to abortion pills like these.

the law could potentially be applied to works of art that simply discuss abortion. She says:

> The college has pulled works of art documenting women speaking honestly about their experiences with pregnancy and abortion. This decision silences their voices and deprives the public of a critical opportunity to engage in a broader conversation about these important topics. It jeopardizes a bedrock First Amendment principle that the state refrain from interfering with expressive activity because it disagrees with a particular point of view.[2]

The Debate over Restricting Expression

In recent years numerous policies of government bodies, schools, and other private organizations have been met with claims of censorship. Free speech advocates warn that censorship is rising at a concerning rate. Joe Cohn, legislative and policy director of the Foundation for Individual Rights and Expression, a nonprofit civil liberties group, says:

> We are seeing tremendous attacks on First Amendment freedoms across the country right now, at all levels of government. Censorship is proliferating, and it's deeply troubling. This year, we're seeing a wave of bills targeting drag performances, where simply being gender nonconforming is enough to trigger the penalty. We're also seeing a wave of bills regulating what can be in public or K–12 school libraries. On college campuses, we have been tracking data about attempts to get faculty members punished or even fired for speech or expression, and the numbers are startling—it's the highest rate that we've seen in our 20 years of existence.[3]

"We are seeing tremendous attacks on First Amendment freedoms across the country right now, at all levels of government. Censorship is proliferating, and it's deeply troubling."[3]

—Joe Cohn, legislative and policy director of the Foundation for Individual Rights and Expression

Those who support legislation and policies restricting speech in certain situations claim these measures protect the public, especially children, from being exposed to harmful ideas, words, and images. "Everybody complains about being censored," says Marjorie Heins, a First Amendment lawyer and founder of the Free Expression Policy Project. "But at the same time, almost everybody wants to silence things that they find to be really offensive or violating their morality."[4]

> "Everybody complains about being censored. But at the same time, almost everybody wants to silence things that they find to be really offensive or violating their morality."[4]
>
> —Marjorie Heins, lawyer and founder of the Free Expression Policy Project

The debate over what should be allowed and what should be censored can confuse the public and those tasked with enforcing these policies. Banning books, legislating what can be taught in classrooms, and blocking social media posts are examples of actions occurring nationwide, and such instances have sparked an intense debate over what censorship is and how it affects people's lives.

CHAPTER ONE

Free Speech and Its Limits

One of the most cherished rights in America is the right to free speech. Freedom of speech protects the right to say things others disagree with, express personal views, or criticize the government. With freedom of speech, Americans can express themselves without fear of being punished, persecuted, or censored. Many believe this right allows citizens to fully participate in the democratic process by speaking out in favor of or against policies that affect individuals and society.

The US Founding Fathers understood the importance of freedom of speech. They had lived under the rule of the English king and Parliament, which shut down colonists' protests of unjust British policies in America. After gaining independence, American legislators protected this right in the First Amendment to the US Constitution, which states, "Congress shall make no law respecting an establishment of religion, or prohibiting the free exercise thereof; or abridging the freedom of speech, or of the press; or the right of the people peaceably to assemble, and to petition the Government for a redress of grievances."[5]

The right to free speech was a reaction to authoritarian rule, but even the Founding Fathers did not expect it to mean that Americans can say whatever they want, whenever they want. The First Amendment does not protect all speech, and over the years, limits to free speech have been accepted in specific circumstances. For example, only fifteen years after gaining independence from Britain, Congress passed the Sedition Act of 1798, which made it a crime to criticize the government with the intent to stir up rebellion. During the Civil War the federal government similarly arrested thousands of antiwar protesters for disloyal speech.

Limits During War

Restrictions on wartime speech continued in the early 1900s. As the United States prepared to enter World War I, Congress passed the Espionage Act (1917) and Sedition Act (1918) to silence dissent and enforce public loyalty. Under these acts the US government blocked the mailing of antiwar newspapers and magazines. Across the country, the government arrested and jailed numerous antiwar protesters, including prominent Socialist Eugene Debs.

Debs was a well-known leader of the Socialist movement in the United States in the early 1900s. He had led several historic labor strikes and had run for president four times as a Socialist Party candidate. Debs was also decidedly against the United States' entering World War I. In June 1918 Debs spoke to a

Free speech is one of the most cherished rights in the United States, and has been since the days of the Founding Fathers. This picture shows protesters exercising their free speech rights.

crowd in a Canton, Ohio, park. "The working class have never yet had a voice in declaring war," he said. "If war is right, let it be declared by the people—you, who have your lives to lose."[6] Within two weeks, he was arrested by US marshals and charged with ten counts of violating the Espionage and Sedition Acts during the Canton speech.

During his trial Debs spoke to the jury. "I believe in free speech, in war as well as in peace," he said. "If the Espionage Law stands, then the Constitution of the United States is dead."[7] However, the jury disagreed and found Debs guilty on three counts, and a judge sentenced him to ten years in prison. Some newspaper editorials applauded the verdict. "His activities in opposition to the war preparation were dangerous," the *Washington Post* declared. "His conviction . . . serves notice to all that disloyalty and sedition, even though masquerading under the guise of free speech, will not be tolerated."[8] Debs appealed his conviction, arguing to the US Supreme Court in 1919 that free speech protected his opinions. He lost that appeal.

Eugene Debs, pictured addressing a crowd, was a well-known leader of the Socialist movement in the United States in the early 1900s.

Clear and Present Danger

The Debs case was decided just one week after the Supreme Court handed down a similar judgment in *Schenck v. United States* (1919). Charles Schenck was a citizen who opposed US involvement in World War I. He mailed thousands of antiwar pamphlets to young, draft-eligible men and encouraged them not to enlist in the military. Schenck was arrested and charged with inciting potential harm. In his defense, Schenck argued that the First Amendment established his freedom of speech rights and protected him from prosecution.

However, the Supreme Court disagreed with Schenck. The court ruled that speech that might encourage violence or lawless action was an exception. The justices reasoned that the risk of injury to others excludes the speech from First Amendment protections. Justice Oliver Wendell Holmes Jr. wrote in the court's majority opinion:

> "The most stringent protection of free speech would not protect a man in falsely shouting fire in a theatre and causing a panic."[9]
>
> —Oliver Wendell Holmes Jr., US Supreme Court justice

The most stringent protection of free speech would not protect a man in falsely shouting fire in a theatre and causing a panic. It does not even protect a man from an injunction against uttering words that may have all the effect of force. . . . The question in every case is whether the words used are used in such circumstances and are of such a nature as to create a clear and present danger that they will bring about the substantive evils that Congress has a right to prevent. It is a question of proximity and degree.[9]

This ruling established a now-famous principle of constitutional law: the "clear and present danger" test. This test is simple. The government cannot restrict speech unless the speech creates a known, immediate threat to public safety. Central to the test is the idea of proximity and degree. This means that if speech

Self-Censorship in Hollywood

In the 1920s several scandals hit Hollywood, including those involving alleged rape and murder. Concerned religious, civic, and political groups called for decency laws to oversee Hollywood. Rather than having to deal with multiple state laws, the motion picture industry decided to self-censor and adopted a set of industry guidelines called the Motion Picture Production Code. The code was also known as the Hays Code after Will Hays, president of the Motion Picture Producers and Distributors of America. The Hays Code was adopted in 1930 and enforced in 1934. It detailed what was acceptable and unacceptable content for motion pictures in the United States and included prohibitions of nudity, suggestive dances, excessive use of liquor, ridicule of religion, lustful kissing, and scenes of sexual passion. The motion picture industry followed the code's guidelines for several decades, until 1968 when it was replaced by the Motion Picture Association of America's film-rating system. Though the rating system is still an industry-regulated code, the movie studios have become more tolerant of what can be shown in movies—as long as viewers can trust that the ratings will accurately alert them to the content that will be on display.

causes an immediately dangerous action, such as yelling "fire" in a crowded theater, the First Amendment does not protect it.

In the following decades, the Supreme Court attempted to find a proper balance between free speech and public safety. Many cases the court heard challenged the government's authority to censor or punish political protest. In each case, the justices refined the "clear and present danger" test. Many decisions recognized a person's right to speak freely, but most decisions imposed some limitations when public safety was involved.

Fighting Words

So-called fighting words are also not protected speech under the First Amendment. Fighting words are words meant to incite violence. In *Chaplinsky v. New Hampshire* (1942), the Supreme Court identified several exceptions to First Amendment speech protections, including obscenities, profane and defamatory speech, and fighting words. The justices defined *fighting words* as those that inflict injury, incite violence, or disturb the peace. They concluded that police have the right to curb the use of fighting words to maintain order.

Over the following decades, the court refined what speech or actions could be considered fighting words. Words used to incite a riot are unprotected, but direct personal insults are not considered fighting words.

Obscenity

Obscene speech is also not protected by the First Amendment. At first the Supreme Court let individual states determine what materials and speech were obscene. However, in the 1950s the court began to hear these cases and examine material to determine how to define obscenity at the federal level.

In 1957 the court heard *Roth v. United States*. Samuel Roth was a New York bookstore owner who sold a publication containing nude photography and routinely mailed the magazine to customers. He was arrested and convicted for sending obscene material through the mail. Roth appealed his case to the Supreme Court, arguing that free speech rights protected him. The Supreme Court upheld his conviction and established the *Roth* test. Under this test, Congress can ban obscene material, defined as material without redeeming social importance. Years later the Supreme Court modified the obscenity test in *Miller v. California* (1973) and defined conditions that jurors must consider before deeming speech or material obscene.

Defamation, Libel, and Slander

Defamation, which includes libel and slander, is also an exception to free speech rights. It basically involves saying or publishing something that damages the reputation or basic human dignity of another person. However, specific standards must be met for this type of speech to be unprotected under the First Amendment. In 1964 the Supreme Court established these standards in *New York Times Company v. Sullivan*.

In this case the *New York Times* published an ad to raise donations to defend civil rights leader Martin Luther King Jr. from perjury charges regarding his tax returns. The ad criticized police in Montgomery, Alabama, for their poor treatment of civil rights protesters. However, the newspaper ad contained errors about, among other things, the number of times King had been arrested previously in Alabama. L.B. Sullivan, the Montgomery police commissioner, pointed to the harsh words and factual errors to claim that he—as supervisor of public safety—was being attacked. He accused the *New York Times* of defamation and filed a libel lawsuit against the newspaper. After a state court jury awarded Sullivan $500,000 in damages, the *New York Times* appealed the decision.

The Supreme Court ruled in favor of the *New York Times* and defined the requirements for defamation to occur. The court determined that in a libel claim, the plaintiff must show that the defendant knew the published statement was false or recklessly published without verifying the statement's accuracy. The court established three conditions to test for libel. First, there must be actual malice, meaning the accused intended to harm another

In a 1964 Supreme Court defamation case involving Martin Luther King (pictured) and Montgomery, Alabama, police, the court defined the criteria necessary for defamation to not fall under free speech protection.

Cross Burning and Free Speech

In 1990 Robert Viktora, a juvenile in St. Paul, Minnesota, made a crude cross and burned it in the fenced yard of a local Black family. He was arrested and charged under a bias-motivated-crime ordinance that outlawed any act that "arouses anger, alarm or resentment in others on the basis of race, color, creed, religion or gender." Viktora's lawyer argued that the ordinance was too broad and content-based, which means it discriminated on the basis of what was said or expressed. Typically, content-based laws are usually found unconstitutional by the courts. In 1992 the US Supreme Court struck down the St. Paul ordinance in *R.A.V. v. City of St. Paul*. The court ruled that the ordinance unconstitutionally prohibited only acts that were designed to arouse anger or outrage over race, gender, or religion. The ordinance did not ban other acts that were also designed to arouse anger or outrage over other issues. In 2003 the court would refine that decision in *Virginia v. Black* and rule that the First Amendment does not protect acts such as cross burning if the purpose is intimidation.

person's reputation. Second, the accused must know the statement is false. And third, there must be actual harm for defamation to occur. If all three conditions are met, the First Amendment does not protect that speech.

Symbolic Speech and Acts of Expression

The Supreme Court has also considered whether symbols or actions can be protected as free speech under the First Amendment. Pictures and symbols are often a powerful way to send a message and spark an emotional response. In *Tinker v. Des Moines Independent Community School District* (1969), the court ruled that public school students had the right to wear black armbands in school to protest the Vietnam War.

In *Texas v. Johnson* (1989), the court ruled that certain acts of expression are considered speech protected under the First Amendment. In 1984 Gregory Johnson burned an American flag in front of city hall in Dallas, Texas. Johnson was protesting President Ronald Reagan's administration and its policies. Johnson was arrested and convicted under a Texas law that prohibited desecration of the US flag. He was sentenced to one year in jail and fined $2,000. The conviction was reversed on appeal, and the case was sent to the US Supreme Court.

In a 5–4 decision, the court sided with Johnson. The justices ruled that his flag burning was a form of speech. Therefore, it was a protected expression under the First Amendment. The fact that others were offended by his expression did not justify banning it. And because there was no violence or intimidation involved with his flag burning, it was not an exception. "If there is a bedrock principle underlying the First Amendment, it is that the Government may not prohibit the expression of an idea simply because society finds the idea itself offensive or disagreeable,"[10] wrote Justice William Brennan in the court's majority opinion.

Free Speech and Private Groups

The First Amendment protects speech from any government censorship at the federal, state, and local levels. It protects from retribution by government officials and entities, such as lawmakers, elected officials, public schools, universities, courts, and police officers. Censorship enacted by any of these groups or individuals is unconstitutional.

However, private citizens, businesses, and organizations are not bound by First Amendment free speech protections. If the government is not involved, private citizens and groups are free to censor without violating the Constitution. This means that private schools can discipline students for speaking out against the administration. A private business can fire an employee for expressing political views at work. And a private media company can refuse to publish views that it does not agree with.

Freedom of speech is a cherished American right. However, over the years, Americans have disagreed about what is meant by speech and where free speech rights begin and end. This disagreement has led to disputes over censorship and when it is acceptable to limit speech in any of its forms.

CHAPTER TWO

Banning Books

In January 2022 the McMinn County School Board in Tennessee voted to remove *Maus: A Survivor's Tale*, a graphic novel about the Holocaust, from its eighth-grade curriculum. The Pulitzer Prize–winning book tells the story of author Art Spiegelman's father's time in a Nazi concentration camp. Parents and teachers complained after the book was added to the school curriculum. Many objected to a few swear words, an image of a partially nude person, and the violence described in the book. At first the school directed staff to redact the book's swear words and the objectionable image. But the school board decided further action was needed. "We don't need to enable or somewhat promote this stuff. It shows people hanging. It shows them killing kids. Why does the educational system promote this kind of stuff? It is not wise or healthy,"[11] said board member Tony Allman.

At the January school board meeting, curriculum supervisor Melasawn Knight defended *Maus* and its depictions of violence. She pointed out that the book was an accurate representation of the Holocaust. "People did hang from trees, people did commit suicide, and people were killed—over six million were murdered,"[12] said Knight.

Despite pleas to keep the book, the school board voted to ban *Maus*. "This board is the arbiter of community standards as it relates to the curriculum in McMinn County schools," said the school board's lawyer, Scott Bennett, after the vote. "At the end of the day, it is this board that has the responsibility to make these decisions."[13]

The decision sparked a public outcry, but the board refused to reconsider the ban. The ban also led Emma Stratton, a McMinn County High School junior, to travel an hour away to buy several

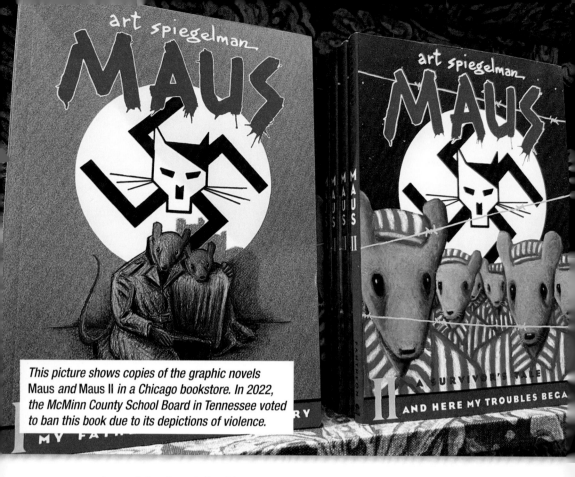

This picture shows copies of the graphic novels Maus and Maus II in a Chicago bookstore. In 2022, the McMinn County School Board in Tennessee voted to ban this book due to its depictions of violence.

copies of the book in Chattanooga. "If they take away this book, what else are they going to take away from us?" said Emma. "They're trying to hide history from us."[14]

A Battle over Books

Parents and educators have battled over the books allowed in schools and libraries for years. Book-ban supporters say banning is necessary to protect children from unsuitable and potentially harmful content. "This is not about banning books; it's about protecting the innocence of our children and letting the parents decide what the child gets rather than having government schools indoctrinate our kids,"[15] says Keith Flaugh, a founder of the Florida Citizens Alliance, a conservative group focused on education. Critics push back and argue that book bans are a form of censorship by those who are trying to silence viewpoints with which they disagree.

One title that has caused much controversy over the years is the semiautobiographical, antiwar, science-fiction novel *Slaughterhouse-Five* by author Kurt Vonnegut. The book tells the story of protagonist Billy Pilgrim amid the horrors of World War II. Pilgrim is a prisoner of war and lives through the bombing of Dresden, Germany. Traumatized, Pilgrim becomes able to travel in time and relive moments in his life.

Since its 1969 publication, *Slaughterhouse-Five* has faced at least eighteen banning attempts in public schools and libraries in the United States. Parents, teachers, and community members objected to the novel's obscene language, depictions of sexual acts, mentions of homosexuality, and what they considered a lack of patriotism. In 1973 a North Dakota school board president burned thirty-two copies of the book in the school's furnace. Some bans were successful—including those in Levittown, New York (1975), North Jackson, Ohio (1979), and Lakeland, Florida (1982). In these cases, the bans were based on claims that the book contained "explicit sexual scenes, violence, and obscene language,"[16] according to the American Library Association.

> "This is not about banning books; it's about protecting the innocence of our children and letting the parents decide what the child gets rather than having government schools indoctrinate our kids."[15]
>
> —Keith Flaugh, a founder of the Florida Citizens Alliance

What Happens When a Book Is Challenged?

When a book is challenged, most school districts and libraries have a process for deciding what to do with the book. For example, when more than one hundred books were challenged in Florida's Escambia County Public Schools, the affected titles were immediately placed in a restricted section until their status could be determined. Students had to present a signed parental permission form to read books in the restricted area. For every challenged book, several different boards—including the School Materials Review Committee, the District Materials Review Committee, and the school board—read the book. Each member of the committee reads the book. They analyze it for literary value and how it complies with state law. If it passes all those reviews, the book can be placed back on the library and classroom shelves. The reviewers also evaluate whether a book is age appropriate for students. The book is returned to the main library if the reviewer and committees approve it. If not approved, it is removed from the school entirely. The process is repeated for each challenged book.

In 1982 the US Supreme Court weighed the book ban against First Amendment rights in the case of *Island Trees School District v. Pico*. In 1975 the Island Trees School District received a complaint from a local parents' group about several books, including *Slaughterhouse-Five*. The complaint alleged that these books were "anti-American, anti-Christian, anti-Semitic, and just plain filthy."[17] The school district removed the books from school libraries in 1976. In response, senior Steven Pico and four other students challenged the school board's decision in federal district court. Pico asserted that the books were removed because they offended the board's social, political, and moral views. The students added that the books had educational value. The Supreme Court sided with Pico based on the First Amendment. The court ruled that the First Amendment implies the right to read. Government entities such as public schools cannot restrict content in a school library simply because the board members disagree with it.

Slaughterhouse-Five, *written by Kurt Vonnegut, who is pictured here in 1977, has faced at least eighteen banning attempts in public schools and libraries in the United States.*

Challenges on the Rise

Before 2020 most challenges to school and library books were initiated by individuals such as parents, teachers, and other community members. Their goal was to remove or restrict access to a single book. They challenged books for a range of reasons. They objected to profanity, sexual content, or violence. Some people challenged books that conflicted with their religious beliefs or that they felt were unsuitable for a particular age group.

Since 2020 calls for book bans have increased. In 2022 the number of attempted book bans set a record, according to the American Library Association (ALA). More than 1,200 challenges were recorded, nearly double the previous total of 729 challenges in 2021. Deborah Caldwell-Stone, director of the ALA's Office for Intellectual Freedom, says that her office has never been so busy, often dealing with multiple reports each day about book challenges. "I've never seen anything like this," says Caldwell-Stone. "The last two years have been exhausting, frightening, outrage-inducing."[18]

An Organized Effort

Not only are the calls for book bans increasing, but the way books are being challenged is also changing. Now more challenges cover multiple titles instead of a single book. In fact, according to the ALA, 90 percent of reported book challenges in 2022 demanded removing or restricting multiple titles. And of those demands, 40 percent aimed to censor more than one hundred books at once.

A 2022 report by PEN America, a free speech advocacy organization, found that at least fifty national groups with branches across the country are behind most of these book challenges. The groups include Moms for Liberty, No Left Turn in Education, and MassResistance, among others. Such organizations initiated at least half of all book challenges, PEN America reports. "The large majority of book bans underway today are not spontaneous, organic expressions of citizen concern. Rather, they reflect the work of a growing number of advocacy organizations that have made demanding censorship of certain books and ideas in schools part of their mission,"[19] write the report's authors.

The organized efforts to ban books have grown since 2020 and are part of a larger movement to restrict school lessons about race, gender identity, and sexual orientation. In many of these cases, there is evidence of an organized effort, which includes using similar presentation strategies and sharing lists of books successfully banned in other schools to help parents raise their own challenges. "Each attempt to ban a book by one of these groups represents a direct attack on every person's constitutionally protected right to freely choose what books to read and what ideas to explore," says Caldwell-Stone. "The choice of what to read must be left to the reader or, in the case of children, to parents. That choice does not belong to self-appointed book police."[20]

> "Each attempt to ban a book . . . represents a direct attack on every person's constitutionally protected right to freely choose what books to read and what ideas to explore."[20]
>
> —Deborah Caldwell-Stone, director of the ALA's Office for Intellectual Freedom

Brian Camenker is the executive director of MassResistance, one of the groups working to remove certain books from schools and libraries. According to Camenker, most books parents and community members object to contain inappropriate sexual content. In their view, books with sexual content, particularly books with LGBTQ themes and content, are considered pornography. Camenker believes this type of sexual content has no place in school libraries. "The LGBT issues, this is not necessarily a healthy behavior for libraries to be promoting on kids. And, and all of them, every one that I see involves sexuality," he says. "The question isn't really, who would want to ban these books, but the question is, who would want them?"[21]

Many people have become increasingly concerned over the organized efforts to ban books and the consequences for students, schools, and libraries. "These groups probably do not necessarily represent a range of beliefs from our democracy," says Jonathan Friedman, the director of PEN America's free expression and education programs and author of the 2022 report. "So they're having an outsized impact in a lot of places on what it is that everybody gets to read. And that, I think, is what's most concerning."[22]

Liberal Challenges to Books in Schools

Book challenges are not limited to conservative voices and groups. For years books have been challenged by people and groups with more liberal viewpoints. For example, two books, *Of Mice and Men* by John Steinbeck and *To Kill a Mockingbird* by Harper Lee, have been challenged for years for their alleged insensitive portrayal of mental illness and race, respectively. In 2020 both books were on the American Library Association's list of the ten most-challenged books. And these books continue to be challenged. In 2022 the school board in the Mukilteo School District in Washington State voted to remove *To Kill a Mockingbird* from the ninth-grade curriculum. The board had received complaints that the book marginalized characters of color, used racial slurs, and celebrated "White saviorhood." The board decided the book would no longer be required reading for students but voted to keep it on the district's list of books approved for school libraries and classrooms.

Fight in Florida

In May 2023, Moms for Liberty, a conservative nonprofit that advocates for parental rights, presented to Florida's Santa Rosa County School Board a list of sixty-five books that it insisted should be removed from the district's schools because of offensive content. The district's current policy allows parents to decide whether their child should have unlimited, limited, or no access to school and classroom libraries.

Founded in 2021, Moms for Liberty uses a team of volunteers to read library books and prepare reports on titles that contain what the organization believes to be concerning—especially sexually explicit—material. "Our goal is to protect our children from those horrible materials that can damage their childhood and their innocence. It's very heartbreaking that the subject is even debatable. It should be just what's bad is bad. Pornography in school libraries is bad, and we want to stop that,"[23] says Mariya Calkins, founder of the Santa Rosa County chapter of Moms for Liberty.

Although Moms for Liberty asserts that it is focused on removing sexually explicit content, some of the books the group wants removed focus on social issues, including race, racism, social justice, and police violence. The Santa Rosa school board has stated that the book challenges will go through the district's established review process before a decision is made.

Federal Lawsuit

The outcome of the book challenges in Santa Rosa County schools may depend on what happens in nearby Escambia County, Florida. In the fall of 2022, the district began removing books from schools after a high school language arts teacher, Vicki Baggett, challenged more than one hundred titles that she described as containing pornography and depiction of child sexual assault. She strongly believes minors should not read these books and wants parents and teachers to pay more attention to what their children are reading. "This is not about banning, this is about making sure that our books, even at the library level, are age-appropriate and content-appropriate. That's it in a nutshell,"[24] she says.

A mother and her daughter join other protesters in Austin, Texas, in 2022, where they read books from a list of books that have been targeted for censorship. In recent years, there have been increasing efforts to ban books in schools and libraries across the United States.

One of the books Baggett challenged was *All Boys Aren't Blue* by George M. Johnson. The book recounts the author's experiences growing up as a Black queer boy. Baggett objected to the book's detailed account of sexual encounters and sexual assault. A review committee recommended keeping the book in the district's high school libraries, but the school board voted to ban it in February 2023 from the district entirely.

In May 2023 PEN America and book publisher Penguin Random House filed a federal lawsuit arguing that the book bans in Escambia County Public Schools were unconstitutional. The plaintiffs claim that public education has a requirement to ensure that students have access to a wide range of topics and viewpoints. They accuse the school board of removing books that discuss race, racism, and LGBTQ identities against the recommendation of the district's book review committee, which they claim violates the First Amendment. The lawsuit also argues that the book bans violate the equal protection clause of the Constitution since many bans target books written by non-White and/or LGBTQ authors. "Books have the capacity to change lives for the better, and students in particular deserve equitable access to a wide range of perspectives," says Nihar Malaviya, chief executive officer (CEO) of Penguin Random House. Malaviya adds, "Censorship, in the form of book bans like those enacted by Escambia County, are a direct threat to democracy and our Constitutional rights."[25]

> "Books have the capacity to change lives for the better, and students in particular deserve equitable access to a wide range of perspectives."[25]
>
> —Nihar Malaviya, CEO of Penguin Random House

Reversing a Ban

In some cases activists have successfully reversed book bans. In 2020 Pennsylvania's Central York School District placed a freeze on more than three hundred antiracist books and resources. At the time, the school board said it had heard from many parents concerned about several titles on the list. The school board put the titles on a list of banned resources.

The move angered many teachers, parents, and students. A group of students from Central York High School's Panther Anti-Racist Union began to hold daily protests in September 2021. Students also joined parents and other community members to discuss their concerns at school board meetings. Their efforts worked. In late September 2022 the school board voted unanimously to reverse the book bans. "It took five high schoolers organizing a peaceful walk-in protest for each day . . . to help make sure that our district heard that they, and many others, did not feel represented. They are heroes and should be celebrated as bastions of American freedom and democracy,"[26] says Ben Hodge, Central York High School theater teacher and cofacilitator for the student Panther Anti-Racist Union.

The battle over books in schools and libraries is not new. However, book challenges are becoming increasingly more common and organized. National and local groups have campaigned to challenge books they do not deem appropriate for the nation's youth. While some support these efforts, others caution that banning books and suppressing different experiences and viewpoints will do more harm than good.

CHAPTER THREE

Controversy in the Classroom

Book bans are one part of the larger debate over restricting class-room conversations and lessons about various subjects, including race, racism, gender identity, and sexual orientation. In recent years more states have proposed legislation that dictates what can and cannot be taught in classrooms from kindergarten to high school. In some cases proposed legislation reaches even further, into college classrooms and public and private employers.

Divisive Concepts

The most recent debate over what material can be presented in classrooms arose during the administration of President Donald Trump. In September 2020 Trump issued an executive order that banned federal contractors and grant recipients from training on "divisive concepts" that primarily relate to gender and race. The administration held that America had made great strides to ensure that all people are treated equally and that assuming the nation will always suffer from institutional racism and sexism simply perpetuates harmful stereotypes. Because they receive federal grants, colleges pondered how Trump's executive order applied to them, and some chose to pause diversity initiatives, talks on racial identity on campus, and other programs that might conflict with the order.

A federal judge halted enforcement of the executive order in December 2020, and President Joe Biden later revoked the order entirely. However, the effects of the order continue to impact legislators in states nationwide. State Republicans have since taken up the issue, prompting a flood of bills hitting state legislatures to restrict what can be taught in schools and workplaces.

Since 2021 state legislatures and local school boards have increasingly taken action to curb or ban discussion and instruction of controversial or divisive subjects in the classroom. In 2022 thirty-six states introduced 137 gag-order bills. Although many of these bills are still working their way through the legislative process, people are concerned about the disturbing trend. "These dangerous attempts to stoke fears and rewrite history not only diminish the injustices experienced by generations of Americans, they prevent educators from challenging our students to achieve a more equitable future,"[27] says National Education Association president Becky Pringle.

New Laws Limit Instruction

To date, only a few of these proposed bills have successfully passed through state legislatures. One is Florida's Parental Rights in Education Act. Signed into law in 2022, the act, commonly referred to as the "Don't Say Gay" law, prohibits classroom instruction on sexual orientation and gender identity for students in kindergarten through third grade. In April 2023 the Florida Board of Education extended the ban to all grades from kindergarten through high school, except when discussing gender and sexual orientation as part of a health course following state-mandated education policy. And in May 2023 Florida governor Ron DeSantis signed another bill that further modified the act by dictating that reproductive health instruction must be age appropriate in sixth through eighth grades. The law does not specify what constitutes age-appropriate content. The 2023 bill also bans teachers and school employees from asking students about or revealing their own preferred pronouns.

Supporters of the act say that it protects children from being taught inappropriate subjects in school. The new laws also protect parents' right to decide what their children learn about sexuality and gender and when they learn it. Republican state senator Clay

Critics worry that proposed legislation to prevent divisive concepts from being taught in schools will mean that people will no longer learn about controversial parts of American history such as slavery. This picture shows a group of African Americans picking cotton near Savannah, Georgia, after the Civil War.

Yarborough, who sponsored the 2023 expansion, explained, "This legislation will protect the rights of parents to have a say in their children's education and ensure that students are not subjected to inappropriate material. . . . Teachers should be able to spend their time focusing on skills that help a child succeed in life, not delving into every social issue or being forced to use language that would violate their personal convictions."[28] Supporters like Republican state representative Joe Harding emphasized that the bills would not ban students from talking about their LGBTQ families or having classroom discussions about LGBTQ history.

Other states are using as a model Florida's legislation and proposing bills to restrict what can be taught in public schools. At least thirty proposed bills have been filed in sixteen states. Two states, Alabama and Arkansas, have already passed similar laws. Alabama's 2022 law bans classroom instruction on gender identity or sexual orientation in public schools for grades kindergarten through fifth grade, while Arkansas's 2023 law bans classroom instruction on these topics before fifth grade.

> "Teachers should be able to spend their time focusing on skills that help a child succeed in life, not delving into every social issue or being forced to use language that would violate their personal convictions."[28]
>
> —Clay Yarborough, Florida state senator

Critics Speak Out

Critics have spoken out against such measures, saying they marginalize LGBTQ people and stifle what teachers and students can discuss. The Florida State Senate minority leader, Democrat Lauren Book says, "This bill insults the professionalism of educators. It takes away freedom of speech, freedom of thought, and freedom to be treated equally in our public schools."[29] Some of Florida's Democratic lawmakers believe the law unfairly targets the LGBTQ community. "What we're doing here is codifying disrespect, just because someone is different than us,"[30] says State Senator Tracie Davis. State Senator Tina Polsky agrees. "Trans is a fact of life. Gay is a fact of life. You can't legislate away the gay, as much as you might try,"[31] she says.

> "[Florida's Parental Rights in Education Act] insults the professionalism of educators. It takes away freedom of speech, freedom of thought, and freedom to be treated equally in our public schools."[29]
>
> —Lauren Book, Florida state senator

Students across Florida have also spoken out against the new law. After the law's passage in 2022, students across the state staged school walkouts to protest the law and reject the claim that it protects impressionable children from harm. "The language and the supporters of the bill and the rhetoric around the bill really shows what this bill is, and it's an attempt to hurt queer people like me,"[32] says Flagler-Palm Coast High School senior Jack Petocz, who led his school's protest.

Critics also point out that these laws are vague, making it difficult to determine "instruction" or "age-appropriate" lessons. "There's no guidance in any of this, none whatsoever, which has made it the wild, wild west,"[33] says Andrew Spar, president of the Florida Education Association. With little guidance, teachers and school officials are left to decide what is acceptable and what is not. "Teachers are wondering, can I put up a rainbow sticker? Can I talk about this LGBTQ+ historical figure? Can I put up a picture of my wife if I'm a woman? That is a big concern, where does the censorship begin and end with these bills?"[34] says Courtnay Avant, legislative counsel for the Human Rights Campaign.

Race, Racism, and American History

Other legislative bills have attempted to restrict what can be taught in classrooms about race, racism, and American history. For example, Georgia passed the Protect Students First Act in 2022, which prohibits instruction in K–12 schools on divisive concepts that pertain to race. The law defines divisive concepts as those that teach "the United States of America is fundamentally racist; an individual, by virtue of his or her race, is inherently or consciously racist or oppressive toward individuals of other races," and "an individual, solely by virtue of his or her race, bears individual responsibility for actions committed in the past by other individuals of the same race."[35] Schools violating the law may be subject to more state oversight, and school superintendents may be suspended.

The Georgia law is one example of a larger movement by conservative lawmakers to restrict how race is taught and discussed in schools. Supporters of these laws say that the restrictions are needed to ensure that parents can control how their children are educated on these sensitive topics.

However, critics have blasted the new laws. Many contend that limiting classroom instruction on race and racism will make history lessons incomplete. "Whether you are white, Black, Hispanic or

Restricting Topics in College

In May 2023 Florida governor Ron DeSantis signed a bill into law that restricts how race and gender can be taught in Florida's public universities and colleges. The bill bans any general education courses that teach "identity politics" or "distort" historical events. It also expanded the study of Western civilization to include instruction on its history and philosophy where possible and requires humanities courses to include Western sources. The new laws also ban higher education institutions from funding diversity programs with state or federal money. Andrew Gothard, president of United Faculty of Florida, a union of faculty members at Florida's public universities, objected to the bill, calling it censorship. "We believe in the free exchange of all ideas, and we reject efforts to control what students get to learn and what professors have the right to teach," Gothard says.

Quoted in Rose Horowitch, "DeSantis Signs Bill Defunding Diversity Programs at Florida Colleges," NBC News, May 15, 2023. www.nbcnews.com.

Students are pictured listening to their teacher. Critics argue that limiting classroom instruction on race and racism will make history lessons incomplete.

Asian—most parents want their children to learn about history the way they learn about math—as accurately as possible,"[36] says Andrea Young, executive director of the ACLU of Georgia.

Banning Critical Race Theory

Much of the controversy over discussing race and racism in schools involves critical race theory (CRT). According to scholars, CRT is a way of understanding how racism throughout American history has shaped public policy and institutions. In their words, CRT acknowledges that social institutions in the United States—such as the criminal justice system, education system, health care system, housing market, and labor market—have had racism embedded in their policies and procedures for decades, which has led to different social and economic outcomes for people of different races.

Yet some people believe that CRT is a divisive theory that pits people of color against White people and thus labels people as inherently "victims" and "oppressors" based on their skin color. Many who view CRT in this way feel that it should not be part of discussions of race and racism in the classroom. These beliefs and fears have sparked heated debates in schools nationwide. They have also pressured states and school boards to ban instruction about racism in classrooms.

As of April 2023, twenty-eight states had passed some measures to restrict the teaching of CRT in schools or government employee training. Another twelve states had restrictions passed in individual cities, counties, or school districts. And several more states had proposed legislation. A few laws and regulations specifically mention CRT. Others propose more general bans and restrictions on discussions of race and racism.

Some of the proposed laws would ban teachers from discussing ideas or facts of history that might cause students discomfort. For example, in Connecticut a bill proposed in 2023 would prevent schools from using a curriculum that makes "any individual feel discomfort, guilt, anguish or any other form of psychological distress on account of the individual's race or sex."[37] A 2022 New Jersey bill would ban instruction on critical race theory, and it would prevent teachers from discussing or assigning any classroom material that promotes "division between, or resentment of, a race, sex, religion, creed, nonviolent political affiliation, social class, or class of people."[38]

> "Whether you are white, Black, Hispanic or Asian—most parents want their children to learn about history the way they learn about math—as accurately as possible."[36]
>
> —Andrea Young, ACLU of Georgia executive director

Critics say that many of these laws are so vague that it is unclear what exactly they cover and what teachers are allowed to discuss. For example, teachers are uncertain whether holding classroom discussions about the establishment of Jim Crow laws—which prevented Black Americans from voting, holding office, or sharing public spaces with White people—would be acceptable or considered a violation of the law. Other complex topics in American history, such as American slavery and Japanese internment during World War II, would also be tricky to navigate under these laws and policies.

Educators fear that in states where these laws are passed, teachers will self-censor their lessons and remove these topics entirely to avoid getting in trouble. Ultimately, they fear it will have a negative impact on student learning. "History teachers cannot adequately teach about the Trail of Tears, the Civil War, and the civil rights movement. English teachers will have to avoid teaching almost any text by an African American author because many of them mention racism to various extents,"[39] says Mike Stein, an English teacher in Tennessee.

The 1619 Project

Another flashpoint in the debate over classroom discussion of race, racism, and American history is "The 1619 Project." From the moment of its publication, the project ignited debate over its accuracy and relevance. Taking its name from the year the first African slaves were brought to North America, the project reexam-

Critics have accused "The 1619 Project" of being inaccurate and misrepresenting history. Florida governor Ron DeSantis—pictured here speaking in Virginia in 2023—spoke publicly against the "The 1619 Project" in 2022.

What Is "The 1619 Project"?

"The 1619 Project" is a series of essays, poems, and multimedia first published in the *New York Times Magazine* in 2019. Its title commemorates the year 1619, when enslaved Africans first arrived in the British colonies in America. The project looks at the impact of slavery on American life, economics, and culture. It also makes a bold claim: that the moment when the first enslaved Africans arrived in the English colonies in 1619 is the country's true origin, instead of the traditionally accepted 1776, the date the colonies declared independence. "No aspect of the country that would be formed here has been untouched by the years of slavery that followed," the project says. "On the 400th anniversary of this fateful moment, it is finally time to tell our story truthfully." In later editions of the magazine, writers and historians added more material to the project. A school curriculum was developed, and by February 2021 more than four thousand teachers from fifty states had reported using it in their classrooms.

Quoted in C.A. Bridges, "What Is 'The 1619 Project' and Why Has Gov. DeSantis Banned It from Florida Schools?," *Tallahassee (FL) Democrat*, January 27, 2023. www.tallahassee.com.

ines how slavery impacted American ideals, the nation's economy, its legal system, and other institutions. Supporters praised the project for providing needed education about how race and racism have shaped America. Christopher Span, a history of education professor at the University of Illinois Urbana-Champaign, has added "The 1619 Project" to his classes. He believes the project "centralizes the longstanding role race, racism, and slavery played in the making of this nation and illustrates how their tenets predate those of freedom and democracy by at least one year."[40]

Critics accused "The 1619 Project" of being inaccurate and misrepresenting history. In several states, Republican lawmakers filed bills to cut state funding to schools and colleges that included lessons from "The 1619 Project" in their curricula. In Florida the board of education specifically banned CRT from any educational curriculum and mentioned "The 1619 Project" by name. In September 2022 Florida governor Ron DeSantis spoke about the bans on CRT and "The 1619 Project" in his state. "We are required to teach slavery, Post-Reconstruction and segregation, civil rights, those are core parts of American history that should be taught, but it should also be taught accurately. For example, 'The 1619 Project' is a CRT version of history, it's supported by *The New York Times*. They want to teach that the American Revolution was fought to protect slavery. And that's false,"[41] he said.

Yet others believe that these bans are a form of censorship. Emerson Sykes and Sarah Hinger, attorneys with the ACLU, write:

> These bills don't just set back progress in addressing systemic issues, they also rob young people of an inclusive education and blatantly suppress speech about race. . . . The First Amendment protects the right to share ideas, including the right of listeners to receive information and knowledge. . . . These bills overstep the government's legitimate authority. Instead of encouraging learning, the bills effectively gag educators and students from talking about issues of the most profound national importance, such as the impact of systemic racism in our society. This is a blatant attempt to suppress speech about race these lawmakers disfavor.[42]

The clash between parents, teachers, and schools over what should be taught in classrooms has sparked intense debates in communities nationwide. People on both sides are passionate about protecting children and preserving free speech in schools. The challenge has been finding an acceptable balance.

CHAPTER FOUR

Censoring Online Speech, Misinformation, and Disinformation

The emergence of the internet has given everyday people the ability to create and publish content online via websites, blogs, social media platforms, and more. These online forums have become the new "town squares" where people gather to debate ideas. Yet the internet's accessibility has also created a new set of problems. Anyone with an internet connection can create content, but there are few gatekeepers to verify the reliability of what is posted online. As a result, the internet has become a new place for misinformation and disinformation to flourish.

Moderating Content Online

An overwhelming majority of Americans (95 percent) believe the spread of false information is a serious problem, according to a 2021 poll by the Pearson Institute and the Associated Press-NORC Center for Public Affairs Research. About 75 percent of those polled believe that social media companies and the people who use them are to blame for false information spreading rampantly online.

According to several 2022 Ipsos polls, most Americans believe that if social media companies created this mess, they should be responsible for cleaning it up. The polls revealed that more than half of respondents wanted social media companies to moderate the content on their platforms. Suggested steps include putting warning labels on misinformation (60 percent), deleting problem posts (62 percent), and suspending (62 percent) or banning (57 percent) problematic accounts. Only 17 percent of Americans wanted tech companies to do nothing and allow people to post whatever they wanted, even if posts contained misinformation or bullying.

While Americans want to slow the spread of misinformation, many believe the government should not get involved with moderating content online. In a separate 2022 Ipsos poll, only 30 percent of Americans supported the government's getting involved with moderating social media content. "Basically, public opinion is giving license to tech companies to curate themselves," says Cliff Young, president of US Public Affairs at Ipsos. "What we see across the board is support for self-action by tech companies."[43]

Rules to Protect Users and Platforms

While most Americans agree that content moderation is needed, how to accomplish that effectively and fairly is unclear. There is general agreement that certain types of content should be removed, such as posts that encourage or incite violence. There is also little debate over removing content that is against the law, such as child pornography and terrorist-sponsored content. But for other content, what to do is not as clear. To help them navigate content moderation, social media companies such as Facebook and the company once called Twitter have established rules for user content. These rules aim to protect users and keep the platforms compliant with laws in the countries where they operate.

Because of the sheer volume of content, social media platforms use artificial intelligence tools to flag content that violates their rules. Sometimes, these tools mistakenly flag harmless content. And other times, these tools do not clearly identify content that should be removed.

For example, Twitter (now rebranded as X) ran into problems in March 2023 when it removed posts that it said violated its policy against violence. The company announced that it had used automated processes to remove more than five thousand tweets and retweets of a poster that promoted a "trans day of vengeance" protest in support of transgender rights. "We do not support tweets that incite violence irrespective of who posts them. 'Vengeance' does not imply peaceful protest. Organizing or support for peaceful protests is ok,"[44] said Ella Irwin, Twitter's head of trust and safety at the time.

However, Twitter's automated system removed posts without considering their context. As a result, tweets that were critical of the protests as well as those that supported the protests were removed. People on both sides protested the removal of posts and accused the platform of censorship. Many people shared the image of the protest flyer to speak out against it. They alleged that they were not promoting violence; they were protesting it. And activists who promoted the "trans day of vengeance" pointed out

People use their smartphones on the subway. Anyone connected to the internet can create content, but because there are few gatekeepers to verify reliability, the internet has become a new place for misinformation and disinformation to flourish.

that it is a meme that has existed for years in the trans community and is not a call for violence. "Context is everything in content moderation, which is why content policies should be based in human rights and applied evenly, not changed rapidly based on public pressure or news cycles,"[45] says Evan Greer, director of the nonprofit liberal advocacy group Fight for the Future.

Accusations of Censorship

Twitter is not the only platform accused of using its role as a content moderator to censor content. A group of LGBTQ video creators filed a federal lawsuit against video streaming site YouTube in 2019, accusing the platform of censoring their content. The video creators said that YouTube's algorithms and human moderators target and remove content that features words common to the LGBTQ community, such as *gay*, *lesbian*, and *bisexual*. The video creators alleged that YouTube's censorship has caused them to lose advertising money. YouTube has denied the claims.

The line between content moderation and censorship gets even murkier when platforms attempt to restrict content that they consider misinformation and disinformation. Identifying misinformation is not always an easy task. And deciding what to do with questionable content can be even more difficult. Facebook's handling of posts

Thoughts on Content Moderation

Matt Mullenweg is the CEO of Automattic, which owns the social networking site Tumblr. Mullenweg explained his view of Tumblr's responsibility for content moderation in December 2022, saying:

> There's a phrase we use for a huge amount of speech, and that is "lawful but awful." It might hurt people's mental health, incite harm, or be really mean, like bullying, but it's not technically illegal. We're a private company, so I guess we could host it if we wanted to, but you need to think about your responsibility to society and to your users. It's as if you were hosting a party. It behooves you to provide a safe environment for everyone there that includes food, water, restrooms, and all those sorts of things. I feel like when you're hosting a social network, it's your responsibility to provide a safe and healthy environment.

Quoted in Nilay Patel, "How to Buy a Social Network, with Tumblr CEO Matt Mullenweg," The Verge, December 13, 2022. www.theverge.com.

related to the origin of COVID-19 is one example of the difficulty platforms face regarding misinformation and what to do about it.

In 2020 as the COVID-19 pandemic was spreading worldwide, President Donald Trump told reporters that he had seen evidence that gave him a high degree of confidence that COVID-19 had started in a lab in Wuhan, China. Trump began to use inflammatory labels such as "China virus"[46] when discussing COVID-19. Many people called out Trump's labels as racist and dismissed the idea that the virus could have come from a Chinese lab leak. When Arkansas Republican senator Tom Cotton said China was not up front with the virus's origins, critics described his comments as supporting a conspiracy theory and promoting misinformation.

In February 2021 Facebook announced that it would remove posts promoting the Wuhan lab leak theory. The social media giant explained that the ban was part of a broader policy update to remove more false claims about COVID-19 and vaccines. "Following consultations with leading health organizations, including the World Health Organization (WHO), we are expanding the list of false claims we will remove to include additional debunked claims about the coronavirus and vaccines,"[47] Facebook said in a statement.

Yet a few months later, Facebook quietly walked back its policy of censoring lab leak theory posts as misinformation. The idea that COVID-19 could have escaped from a Chinese lab was increasingly being accepted by experts as possible, including Robert Redfield, the former chief of the Centers for Disease Control and Prevention. In effect, Facebook admitted that the millions of posts it had removed in the past few months had been taken down in error. Many people pointed to the mistake as an example of Facebook censoring speech on its platform.

The role of social media companies in deciding what people can and cannot say online has sparked intense debate. Some people believe that platforms should be doing more content moderation to reduce misinformation, racism, and other types of hateful content online. Yet those lines are often not clearly defined, as Facebook's handling of the lab leak theory shows. And that can

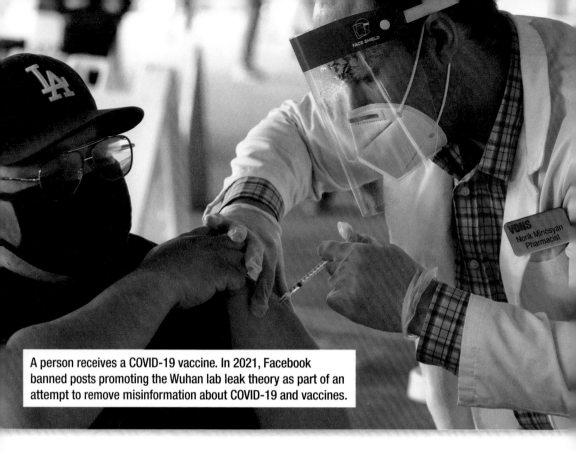

A person receives a COVID-19 vaccine. In 2021, Facebook banned posts promoting the Wuhan lab leak theory as part of an attempt to remove misinformation about COVID-19 and vaccines.

lead to claims of censorship and accusations that social media companies control who has a voice in online conversations.

However, companies like Facebook are not government entities. As a result, they can decide the rules for their platforms' users. There are times when platforms must step in and moderate content, keep discussions civil, remove hate speech, and sometimes stop the spread of misinformation. Roger Entner, a technology and telecommunications analyst, says:

> When it comes to freedom of speech, we have to remember that the First Amendment protects us and Facebook from government interference regarding our speech. It does not protect us from the interference from private parties. It's Facebook's platform and it has total freedom to allow whatever speech it deems appropriate or not, just like you and me can determine what speech is allowed in our house.[48]

Power over Political Speech

The issue of censorship becomes thornier when political speech is involved. Although social media companies have the right to create rules for users on their platforms, they have been accused of political bias and of using their power to promote views they support and suppress views with which they disagree. This issue was highlighted in January 2021 when several online platforms, including Google, Twitter, and Facebook, decided they no longer wanted Donald Trump on their platforms. They announced they were suspending or removing Trump's accounts. They blamed his repeated posting of misinformation and incitement of violence as reasons to shut down his accounts.

Many Trump critics were pleased with the decision to remove Trump's voice from social media. Jonathan Greenblatt, CEO of the Anti-Defamation League, called Twitter's action an "excellent step. A fitting end to a legacy of spewing hate and vitriol. President Trump incited the violent riots at the Capitol using social media & paid the price."[49]

However, others felt uneasy about social media companies' power over online speech. Kate Ruane, a senior legislative coun-

> "It's Facebook's platform and it has total freedom to allow whatever speech it deems appropriate or not, just like you and me can determine what speech is allowed in our house."[48]
>
> —Roger Entner, technology and telecommunications analyst

Elon Musk and Twitter

In 2022 billionaire Elon Musk purchased social media giant Twitter. He explained that he wanted to buy the social media platform and allow it to become a place where users can express themselves freely. He explains his approach, saying "Is someone you don't like allowed to say something you don't like? And if that is the case, then we have free speech." Musk adds that under his ownership, Twitter will be very hesitant to delete content or issue permanent bans, aiming to permit all legal speech. However, when required by a country's laws, Musk notes that Twitter moderators would take down illegal content. Critics have worried that Musk's plans to promote free speech will mean an end to the regulations that Twitter once had in place to limit misinformation and harassing speech.

Quoted in Pristine Villarreal, "Elon Musk Says Twitter Has 'No Actual Choice' About Government Censorship Requests," NBC Palm Springs, May 29, 2023. https://nbcpalmsprings.com.

sel at the ACLU, expressed concern that Trump's suspension from social media could set a dangerous precedent for tech companies to silence other voices. Ruane said in a statement:

> For months, President Trump has been using social media platforms to seed doubt about the results of the election and to undermine the will of voters. We understand the desire to permanently suspend him now, but it should concern everyone when companies like Facebook and Twitter wield the unchecked power to remove people from platforms that have become indispensable for the speech of billions— especially when political realities make those decisions easier. President Trump can turn [to] his press team or Fox News to communicate with the public, but others—like many Black, Brown, and LGTBQ activists who have been censored by social media companies—will not have that luxury.[50]

Too Much Influence?

Concerns over big tech's ability to censor and influence political stories emerged again over a story about a laptop allegedly belonging to President Joe Biden's son, Hunter Biden. Before the 2020 presidential election, the *New York Post*, a conservative newspaper, published a story indicating that this laptop contained emails detailing shady business dealings. In October 2020, weeks before the election, social media giants Facebook and Twitter moved quickly to limit the spread of the laptop story. Facebook used its algorithms to restrict sharing and to push the story down in users' feeds. Twitter blocked users from sharing the *New York Post* story.

At the time, the platforms explained their decisions, noting that the story was unverified and that they had been warned by the Federal

"It should concern everyone when companies like Facebook and Twitter wield the unchecked power to remove people from platforms that have become indispensable for the speech of billions."[50]

—Kate Ruane, senior legislative counsel at the ACLU

44

Prior to the 2020 presidential election, Twitter moved to limit the spread of a story about a laptop allegedly belonging to Joe Biden's son. This picture shows US Representatives James Comer (left), and Jim Jordan at a 2023 hearing investigating the issue.

Bureau of Investigation (FBI) about potential foreign interference and misinformation before the election. They insisted their actions were motivated by the desire to stop the spread of false information on their platforms.

However, critics blasted the social media platforms for suppressing the story. Republican leaders saw the moves as big tech companies using their influence to bury a news report from a major news outlet to influence an election.

Although some questions about the laptop story remained, another newspaper, the *Washington Post*, later authenticated portions of the story in 2022. In a February 2023 hearing before the US House of Representatives Oversight Committee, Republican lawmakers accused Twitter of working with the Biden campaign and the FBI to censor the laptop story. At the hearing, committee chair James Comer of Kentucky said:

> Twitter . . . was a private company the federal government
> used to accomplish what it constitutionally cannot: limit the
> free exercise of speech. Immediately following the story's

publication, America witnessed a coordinated campaign by social media companies, mainstream news, and the intelligence community to suppress and delegitimize the existence of Hunter Biden's laptop and its contents.[51]

Twitter officials admitted at the hearing that they had made a mistake in censoring the story. "I believe Twitter erred in this case because we wanted to avoid repeating the mistakes of 2016,"[52] said Yoel Roth, Twitter's former head of trust and safety. However, they insisted that Biden's campaign or other government agencies had not been involved in the decision to censor the story.

States Propose New Laws

In response to what they viewed as bias against conservative political views, a few states, like Florida and Texas, passed new laws that banned social media platforms from censoring certain posts. In Florida a 2021 state law banned social media platforms from censoring posts by elected officials, political candidates, or major news organizations. And in Texas, a 2021 law banned social media platforms from censoring users' posts based on their political viewpoints. Other states are considering similar bills.

Both laws have been challenged in the courts. In Florida the US Court of Appeals for the Eleventh Circuit struck down most of the Florida law as unconstitutional. But in Texas the US Court of Appeals for the Fifth Circuit sided with Texas in 2022 and upheld the state's law. "Today we reject the idea that corporations have a freewheeling First Amendment right to censor what people say,"[53] the court said. With the two appellate courts issuing conflicting rulings about the rights of companies that host their users' speech, the issue will most likely make its way to the US Supreme Court to determine how to apply the First Amendment to social media.

CHAPTER FIVE

The Debate over Cancel Culture

Throughout history, people have challenged each other's views. Modern technology, including the internet and social media, have made it easier to call out others for their behavior or words and rally a group of people to silence, or "cancel," those they believe have done wrong. While some believe this is a way to hold people accountable for their words and actions, others believe that such a "cancel culture" is being used as censorship.

What Is Cancel Culture?

The phrase *cancel culture* began to appear around 2017 and was linked to the idea of "canceling" celebrities for problem behavior or statements. Meredith Clark, a media studies professor at the University of Virginia, described cancel culture in 2018 as an act of withdrawing support from a person whose actions or expressions are no longer welcome or tolerated. "To me, it's ultimately an expression of agency. To a certain extent: I really do think of it like a breakup and a taking back of one's power,"[54] she said.

At the time, cancel culture was linked to the #MeToo movement, an awareness movement around the issues of sexual harassment and abuse of women that grew in 2017 in response to news reports of sexual abuse by film producer Harvey Weinstein. Many women started sharing their stories of sexual harassment and abuse, and the accused were quickly condemned. This practice of calling someone out for bad behavior, often online, quickly grew in popularity. Anyone online could participate in cancel culture's public shaming, and the internet amplified their voices.

Celebrities found themselves being canceled for a range of reasons. Some were called out, condemned, and canceled for alleged criminal activity. For example, actor Kevin Spacey was called out when multiple accusations of sexual harassment, assault, and misconduct involving cast members and underage boys became public. Although he was not convicted of a crime as of 2023, the controversy led to Spacey's being fired from his hit Netflix show, *House of Cards*. His participation in upcoming movies was canceled, and his agents and publicist dropped him. Spacey was also ordered to pay $31 million to the *House of Cards* producers for violating Netflix's sexual harassment policy. Since then, Spacey has struggled to regain his career.

Kevin Spacey is pictured arriving at the US District Courthouse in New York City in 2022. As a part of cancel culture, Spacey was called out when accusations of sexual harassment, assault, and misconduct became public.

Students Hold a Different View

College administrators emphasize that students must voice their views in a way that encourages constructive dialogue, but many students disagree. A 2023 survey of Princeton University students found that over 75 percent of respondents said it was sometimes acceptable to stop a campus speaker by shouting over them. In the same survey, 43 percent of students thought blocking other students from attending events they disagreed with was acceptable. And 16 percent said using violence to stop a controversial speaker would be justified. "Our survey shows more needs to be done because most students neither support or understand free speech," says Edward Yingling, a cofounder of Princetonians for Free Speech.

Quoted in Neirin Gray Desai, "Three Quarters of Princeton Students Say It's Acceptable to Shout Down Campus Speakers They Disagree with—While 16% Agree with Using Violence to Stop a Speech, After Conservative Judge Was Ambushed by Stanford Law Students and Dean," *Daily Mail* (London), June 8, 2023. www.dailymail.co.uk.

Yet other celebrities were similarly canceled for lesser offenses, such as saying something another person disagreed with. Actor Gina Carano, a star of Disney's *The Mandalorian* television series, enraged some fans with political social media posts. In 2021 she tweeted, "Most people today don't realize that to get to the point where Nazi soldiers could easily round up thousands of Jews, the government first made their own neighbors hate them simply for being Jews. How is that any different from hating someone for their political views?"[55] The tweet was widely shared, and the hashtag #FireGinaCarano began to trend on Twitter. In reaction, Disney cut ties with Carano, and her management company dropped her.

Anyone Can Be Canceled

Cancel culture expanded beyond celebrities into the lives of everyday individuals. People from all backgrounds were held accountable for what they did and said online. For example, videos of people spewing racist or other offensive public rants spread online. Social media users shared the videos and called for accountability for the offensive behavior. And as a result, many people in the videos faced real-life consequences for their actions. In one video, a White woman walking her dog called the police on a Black bird-watcher in New York's Central Park, although the man had done nothing wrong. Social media users called out the woman's behavior as racist. Eventually, she was fired from her job, was charged with a misdemeanor for filing a false police report, and temporarily lost custody of her dog. "What happened to [the woman] was public accountability, because her actions were harmful,"[56] says Shanita Hubbard, chair of a National Association of Black Journalists task force.

Rush to Cancel

However, others believe the rush to cancel a person is misguided. Humans are not perfect; everyone has made mistakes at some point. Canceling or removing someone from public or private life because they have said or done something deemed offensive leaves little room for people to learn from their mistakes and become better people. British author Matt Haig says:

> Canceling people pushes them away and makes them more likely to find spaces were bad views are the norm. Obviously, if someone has been convicted of, say, violence or sexual assault, then they need to be punished, but cancel culture isn't that. Cancel culture, as I see it, involves the shutting down of different perspectives and treating people like mere disposable artifacts in the cultural economy.[57]

In some cases people are being shamed online for statements or behavior deemed offensive that occurred decades ago. For example, in 2020 the Boeing Company's communications chief Niel Golightly was forced out of the company after an employee filed a complaint about an article the former US military pilot had written stating his view that women should not serve in combat. The article in question was written thirty-three years earlier.

Some suggest that a more effective approach would be challenging a person's questionable views or behaviors without canceling them. Not canceling a person gives him or her the room to

Actress and activist Jameela Jamil is pictured here at an event in North Hollywood in 2019. Jamil has spoken out against cancel culture.

grow and learn from mistakes. Actress and activist Jameela Jamil has spoken out against cancel culture and instead supports being challenged, without being canceled, for her actions. "Being called out has made me a better person," she wrote on Instagram. "Not being canceled has enabled me to be accountable, learn from my mistakes, and go on to share those lessons with others and do good with my privilege. Most of us have the potential to do that."[58]

Cancel Culture and Self-Censoring

Free speech protects the right to call out others for what they say or do. Yet when people are canceled for having unpopular views, cancel culture can become hostile to free speech. The First Amendment only protects Americans against the government's censoring of speech; it does not apply to what private citizens do. But some maintain that cancel culture does affect free expression. Free expression and public debate suffer if people do not speak their minds because they fear being canceled.

One example of this occurred in 2020 when David Shor, a polling researcher, sent a tweet summarizing an academic paper from Princeton that compared the effects of violent and nonviolent protests on election turnout. On Twitter, a progressive activist criticized Shor's tweet as minimizing Black grief and rage. More criticism of Shor and accusations of racism appeared online. The next day Shor apologized for the tweet. However, after many demanded that Shor lose his job, his employer, Civis Analytics, fired him. Although the company refused to discuss the reason behind Shor's firing, the timing was difficult to ignore. As a result, people like Shor may self-censor for fear of retaliation by people with differing views. "For all the tolerance and enlightenment that modern society claims, Americans are losing hold of a fundamental right as citizens of a free country: the right to speak their minds and voice their opinions in public without fear of being shamed or shunned,"[59] wrote the *New York Times* in 2022.

Jamil agrees that cancel culture holds people back from expressing their views. In 2020 Jamil said she knew many celebrities who wanted to speak out about the Black Lives Matter movement but were afraid to do so because of cancel culture. She said the potential to be boycotted because they might say something wrong caused these celebrities to remain silent about their support for antiracism causes. "There are people so much more powerful than me who could do so much good, but they're scared of being canceled," Jamil said in 2020. "I know this because I speak to them on a daily basis, and they all want to help, but they're so afraid of getting something wrong."[60]

No matter what one thinks of cancel culture, Americans believe that it affects what they say. A large number of Americans (55 percent) report not feeling free to express their views, according to a 2022 poll by the *New York Times* and Siena College. And most Americans (84 percent) believe that some citizens not exercising their freedom of speech in everyday situations is either a very or somewhat serious problem. "Free speech, a cornerstone of our democracy, is under assault according to everyday Americans," says Siena College Research Institute director Don Levy. "Over half have held their tongue over the last year be-

Fighting Censorship on Campus

In the fall of 2022, Pennsylvania State University officials canceled a comedy event featuring controversial conservative figure and Proud Boys founder Gavin McInnes. Officials had initially planned to allow the event to occur on campus, but they reversed their decision after a demonstration protesting the event turned violent. People who disagreed with the event celebrated its cancellation. However, officials—including university president Neeli Bendapudi—condemned the violence as restricting free speech and generating more publicity for the controversial speaker. A few months later, in April 2023, Bendapudi released a short video statement to address the topic of controversial speakers visiting the university's campuses. In the video, Bendapudi defended the First Amendment and spoke about why the university should allow speakers with controversial views, even if their views were seen by some as hateful and could potentially offend some students, faculty, and staff. "For centuries, higher education has fought against censorship and for the principle that the best way to combat speech is with more speech. To combat bad ideas is with better ideas," said Bendapudi.

Quoted in Ingrid Jacques, "Free Speech Under Attack: 'Triggered' Students Mob Athlete Who Spoke About Women's Sports," *USA Today*, April 21, 2023. www.usatoday.com.

cause they were afraid of retaliation, being harshly criticized or in order to avoid conflict."[61] Levy notes that their fears of criticism and retaliation may partly be justified. He says:

> Not only do a majority of Americans say that they restrict their free expression, but 22% admit to retaliating against or harshly criticizing another person because of something that they said, and nearly half, 44%, think that people that they know have not told them what they were thinking in response to a comment so as to avoid conflict. . . . Our survey describes a country that rather than being a marketplace of ideas, is one in which many of us walk on eggshells afraid of how others will respond to our opinions or simply to "not get into it."[62]

Mob Censorship

Another phenomenon that impacts free speech, mob censorship, has been increasing in recent years, particularly on college campuses. This type of censorship often takes the form of students gathering to heckle and drown out speakers with whom they disagree. One example of this occurred at the State University of New York at Albany in April 2023. Conservative writer and podcast host Ian Haworth was invited to speak on campus by the school's chapter of Turning Point USA, a conservative group. Some students opposed Haworth's invitation and accused him of being transphobic. They sent social media posts and hung posters asking students to protest Haworth's event.

On the day of the speaking event, protesting students filled the meeting room where Haworth was scheduled to speak and shouted profane chants. At one point, the students danced in a conga line. The president of the university's Turning Point USA chapter, Avery Middendorf, tried to speak, but students shouted over him. After more than an hour of relentless chants and shouting, campus police canceled the event. "I was quite disappointed," Middendorf says. "They got what they wanted: They didn't want the speaker on campus in the first place; they got their way."[63]

This type of protest is becoming more common on college campuses. "Students have gone from holding signs, debating, questioning (their opponents)—really debating the issues—to shouting them down," says Zach Greenberg, senior program officer at the Foundation for Individual Rights and Expression in Philadelphia. "I think it really just shows a lack of knowledge about a free-speech culture." Instead of shouting to overwhelm people with different views, Greenberg suggests that students organize a counter event to highlight the opposing viewpoint or prepare questions to ask the speaker and engage in a civil debate. "You do not have a free-speech right to drown out someone else," he says. "We want groups there debating the issues. This act of silencing—that's not very persuasive."[64]

Nico Perrino, executive vice president of the Foundation for Individual Rights and Expression, agrees that this type of disruptive protest should not be accepted. "Shouting down speakers is

> "Shouting down speakers is just like any other form of censorship: It's the few deciding for the many what they can hear."[65]
>
> —Nico Perrino, executive vice president of the Foundation for Individual Rights and Expression

Protests by high school and college students are relatively common in the United States. For example, this picture shows a 2018 gun violence protest at a school in New York. Often, however, opponents silence protesters through mob censorship.

just like any other form of censorship: It's the few deciding for the many what they can hear. Protesters have every right to engage in peaceful, non-disruptive protest. But they do not have the right to take over someone else's event and make it their own,"[65] he says.

The right to speak one's mind freely has been one of the most cherished American rights. The First Amendment is clear that the government may not interfere with this right, except in a few widely accepted circumstances. However, what should be protected as free speech has become increasingly unclear as new efforts to ban books, limit classroom discussions, and remove online content have emerged. Exactly when these efforts cross the line and become censorship remains hotly debated among Americans. Yet many agree that the debate is essential to American democracy. According to the *New York Times* editorial board, "Free expression isn't just a feature of democracy; it is a necessary prerequisite."[66]

SOURCE NOTES

Introduction: Laws That Limit Expression

1. Quoted in Rebecca Boone, "Experts Say Attacks on Free Speech Are Rising Across the U.S.," *PBS NewsHour*, March 15, 2023. www.pbs.org.
2. Quoted in American Civil Liberties Union, "ACLU, NCAC Oppose Removal of Abortion-Related Art from Exhibition at Idaho College Art Gallery," March 3, 2023. www.aclu.org.
3. Quoted in Boone, "Experts Say Attacks on Free Speech Are Rising Across the U.S."
4. Quoted in Thomas Germain, "Actually, Everyone Loves Censorship. Even You," Gizmodo, February 22, 2023. https://gizmodo.com.

Chapter One: Free Speech and Its Limits

5. Quoted in Constitution Annotated, "Constitution of the United States: First Amendment." https://constitution.congress.gov.
6. Quoted in Erick Trickey, "When America's Most Prominent Socialist Was Jailed for Speaking Out Against World War I," *Smithsonian*, June 15, 2018. www.smithsonianmag.com.
7. Quoted in Trickey, "When America's Most Prominent Socialist Was Jailed for Speaking Out Against World War I."
8. Quoted in Trickey, "When America's Most Prominent Socialist Was Jailed for Speaking Out Against World War I."
9. *Schenck v. United States*, 249 U.S. 47 (1919).
10. *Texas v. Johnson*, 491 U.S. 397 (1989).

Chapter Two: Banning Books

11. Quoted in David Corn, "The Inside Story of the Banning of 'Maus.' It's Dumber than You Think," *Mother Jones*, February 1, 2022. www.motherjones.com.
12. Quoted in Sophie Kasakove, "The Fight over 'Maus' Is Part of a Bigger Cultural Battle in Tennessee," *New York Times*, March 4, 2022. www.nytimes.com.
13. Quoted in Kasakove, "The Fight over 'Maus' Is Part of a Bigger Cultural Battle in Tennessee."
14. Quoted in Kasakove, "The Fight over 'Maus' Is Part of a Bigger Cultural Battle in Tennessee."
15. Quoted in Elizabeth A. Harris and Alexandra Alter, "A Fast-Growing Network of Conservative Groups Is Fueling a Surge in Book Bans," *New York Times*, December 12, 2022. www.nytimes.com.
16. Quoted in American Library Association, "Banned & Challenged Classics." www.ala.org.
17. Quoted in Bill of Rights Institute, "*Island Trees School District v. Pico* (1982)," 2023. https://billofrightsinstitute.org.

18. Quoted in Hillel Italie, "Book Ban Attempts Reach Record High in 2022, American Library Association Report Says," *PBS NewsHour*, March 23, 2023. www.pbs.org.
19. Jonathan Friedman and Nadine Farid Johnson, "Banned in the USA: The Growing Movement to Censor Books in Schools," PEN America, September 19, 2022. https://pen.org.
20. Quoted in American Library Association, "American Library Association Reports Record Number of Demands to Censor Library Books and Materials in 2022," March 22, 2023. www.ala.org.
21. Quoted in Eesha Pendharkar, "Who's Behind the Escalating Push to Ban Books? A New Report Has Answers," Education Week, September 19, 2022. www.edweek.org.
22. Quoted in Pendharkar, "Who's Behind the Escalating Push to Ban Books?"
23. Quoted in Brittany Misencik, "Book Ban Controversy Comes to Santa Rosa as Moms for Liberty Seeks Removal of 65 Books," *Pensacola (FL) News Journal*, May 24, 2023. www.pnj.com.
24. Quoted in Brittany Misencik, "100+ 'Questionable' Books Placed in Restricted Section While Escambia Schools Review Them," *Pensacola (FL) News Journal*, October 4, 2022. www.pnj.com.
25. Quoted in Brandon Girod, "PEN America, Penguin Random House Sue Florida School District over Book Ban. What We Know," *Pensacola (FL) News Journal*, May 17, 2023. www.pnj.com.
26. Quoted in Beth Greenfield, "High School Activists Get Controversial Book Ban Reversed in Pennsylvania: 'They Are Heroes,'" Yahoo! September 21, 2021. www.yahoo.com.

Chapter Three: Controversy in the Classroom

27. Quoted in Tim Walker, "Educators Fight Back Against Gag Orders, Book Bans and Intimidation," National Education Association, July 28, 2022. www.nea.org.
28. Quoted in WMNF, "Florida's Controversial Don't Say Gay/Parental Rights in Education Law Is Set to Expand," May 4, 2023. www.wmnf.org.
29. Quoted in WMNF, "Florida's Controversial Don't Say Gay/Parental Rights in Education Law Is Set to Expand."
30. Quoted in WMNF, "Florida's Controversial Don't Say Gay/Parental Rights in Education Law Is Set to Expand."
31. Quoted in WMNF, "Florida's Controversial Don't Say Gay/Parental Rights in Education Law Is Set to Expand."
32. Quoted in Matt Lavietes, "Florida Students Stage School Walkouts over 'Don't Say Gay' Bill," NBC News, March 3, 2022. www.nbcnews.com.
33. Quoted in WUSF Public Media, "Other States Are Copying Florida's Efforts to Ban the Teaching of Gender Identity," March 26, 2023. https://wusf news.wusf.usf.edu.
34. Quoted in WUSF Public Media, "Other States Are Copying Florida's Efforts to Ban the Teaching of Gender Identity."

35. Quoted in Tina Burnside and Devan Cole, "Georgia Gov. Kemp Signs Bill into Law That Limits Discussions About Race in Classrooms," CNN, April 28, 2022. www.cnn.com.
36. Quoted in Burnside and Cole, "Georgia Gov. Kemp Signs Bill into Law That Limits Discussions About Race in Classroom."
37. State of Connecticut General Assembly, "Proposed Bill No. 280," 2023. www.cga.ct.gov.
38. New Jersey Senate Bill 598 (introduced 2022).
39. Quoted in Stephen Sawchuk, "What Is Critical Race Theory, and Why Is It Under Attack?," Education Week, May 18, 2021. www.edweek.org.
40. Quoted in Marybeth Gasman, "What History Professors Really Think About 'The 1619 Project,'" *Forbes*, June 3, 2021. www.forbes.com.
41. Quoted in C.A. Bridges, "What Is 'The 1619 Project' and Why Has Gov. DeSantis Banned It from Florida Schools?," *Tallahassee (FL) Democrat*, January 27, 2023. www.tallahassee.com.
42. Emerson Sykes and Sarah Hinger, "State Lawmakers Are Trying to Ban Talk About Race in Schools," American Civil Liberties Union, May 14, 2021. www.aclu.org.

Chapter Four: Censoring Online Speech, Misinformation, and Disinformation

43. Quoted in Ian Sherr, "Social Media Should Censor Itself, Without Government Intervention, Most Americans Say," CNET, February 14, 2022. www.cnet.com.
44. Quoted in CBS News, "Twitter Removes Tweets About 'Trans Day of Vengeance,'" March 30, 2023. www.cbsnews.com.
45. Quoted in CBS News, "Twitter Removes Tweets About 'Trans Day of Vengeance.'"
46. Quoted in Katie Rogers, "Trump Defends Using 'Chinese Virus' Label, Ignoring Growing Criticism," *New York Times*, March 18, 2020. www.nytimes.com.
47. Facebook, "An Update on Our Work to Keep People Informed and Limit Misinformation About COVID-19," May 26, 2021. https://about.fb.com.
48. Quoted in Peter Suciu, "Social Media About Face: Facebook Won't Remove Claims Covid Was Man-Made," *Forbes*, May 28, 2021. www.forbes.com.
49. Quoted in Brian Fung, "Twitter Bans President Trump Permanently," CNN, January 9, 2021. www.cnn.com.
50. Quoted in Natalie Colarossi, "ACLU Counsel Warns of 'Unchecked Power' of Twitter, Facebook After Trump Suspension," *Newsweek*, January 9, 2021. www.newsweek.com.
51. Quoted in Shannon Bond, "Ex-Twitter Officials Reject GOP Claims of Government Collusion," NPR, February 8, 2023. www.npr.org.
52. Quoted in Bond, Ex-Twitter Officials Reject GOP Claims of Government Collusion."

53. Quoted in Jesus Vidales, "Texas Social Media 'Censorship' Law Goes into Effect After Federal Court Lifts Block," Texas Tribune, September 16, 2022. www.texastribune.org.

Chapter Five: The Debate over Cancel Culture

54. Quoted in Jonah E. Bromwich, "Everyone Is Cancelled," *New York Times*, June 28, 2018. www.nytimes.com.
55. Quoted in Brad Hamilton, "14 Celebrity Members of the Canceled Club: Where Are They Now?," Page Six, April 9, 2022. https://pagesix.com.
56. Quoted in Rachel E. Greenspan, "How 'Cancel Culture' Quickly Became One of the Buzziest and Most Controversial Ideas on the Internet," Insider, August 6, 2020. www.insider.com.
57. Quoted in Ella Alexander, "Cancel Culture: A Force for Good or a Threat to Free Speech?," *Harper's Bazaar*, July 14, 2020. www.harpersbazaar.com.
58. Quoted in *Harper's Bazaar*, "Jameela Jamil Says Stars Are 'Scared' to Speak Out over Black Lives Matter," June 30, 2020. www.harpersbazaar.com.
59. *New York Times*, "America Has a Free Speech Problem," March 18, 2022. www.nytimes.com.
60. Quoted in *Harper's Bazaar*, "Jameela Jamil Says Stars Are 'Scared' to Speak Out over Black Lives Matter."
61. Quoted in Siena College Research Institute, "84% Say Americans Being Afraid to Exercise Freedom of Speech Is a Serious Problem," March 21, 2022. https://scri.siena.edu.
62. Quoted in Siena College Research Institute, "84% Say Americans Being Afraid to Exercise Freedom of Speech Is a Serious Problem."
63. Quoted in Kathleen Moore, "UAlbany Students Shout Down Conservative Speaker," *Albany (NY) Times Union*, April 6, 2023. www.timesunion.com.
64. Quoted in Moore, "UAlbany Students Shout Down Conservative Speaker."
65. Nico Perrino, "Nico Perrino: Heckling Is Not an Exercise of Free Speech," *Pittsburgh (PA) Post Gazette*, April 19, 2023. www.post-gazette.com.
66. *New York Times*, "Censorship Is the Refuge of the Weak," September 10, 2022. www.nytimes.com.

ORGANIZATIONS AND WEBSITES

American Civil Liberties Union (ACLU)
www.aclu.org
The ACLU is a nonprofit organization that works to defend and preserve the individual rights and liberties guaranteed to every person by the Constitution and US laws. Its website provides information about freedom of speech and censorship.

Foundation for Individual Rights and Expression
www.thefire.org
The Foundation for Individual Rights and Expression works to defend the individual rights of all Americans to free speech and free thought. Its website provides the latest research, news, and information about free speech.

Free Speech Center
www.mtsu.edu/first-amendment
The Free Speech Center at Middle Tennessee State University is a nonprofit public policy center dedicated to promoting education, information sharing, and engagement concerning the First Amendment. Its website has articles, news, and other information related to the First Amendment.

National Constitution Center
https://constitutioncenter.org
The National Constitution Center is the leading platform for constitutional education. Its website provides the full text of the Constitution and its amendments, as well as a library of Supreme Court cases concerning constitutional issues.

PEN America
https://pen.org
PEN America is a nonprofit organization that works to defend and celebrate free expression in the United States and worldwide. Its website has information and news about book bans, censorship, and related issues.

Tracking Global Online Censorship
www.onlinecensorship.org
Tracking Global Online Censorship is an information site and tool created by the nonprofit digital rights organization Electronic Frontier Foundation. The online censorship site provides information about how and why social media platforms remove users' posts, how users can appeal these takedown decisions, and how the practice affects freedom of expression all over the world.

FOR FURTHER RESEARCH

Books

Anna Maria Johnson, *Freedom of Speech*. New York: Cavendish Square, 2020.

Meryl Loonin, *Banned Books: The Controversy over What Students Read*. San Diego, CA: ReferencePoint, 2023.

Jonah Lyon, *Pros and Cons: Social Media Censorship*. Ann Arbor, MI: Cherry Lake, 2023.

Leonard S. Marcus, *You Can't Say That! Writers for Young People Talk About Censorship, Free Expression, and the Stories They Have to Tell*. Somerville, MA: Candlewick, 2021.

Ian Rosenberg, *Free Speech Handbook: A Practical Framework for Understanding Our Free Speech Protections*. New York: First Second, 2021.

Gary Wiener, *The New Censorship*. New York: Greenhaven, 2023.

Internet Sources

Daniel Buck, "Book Curation Is Not Censorship," *National Review*, April 2, 2023. www.nationalreview.com.

New York Times, "America Has a Free Speech Problem," March 18, 2022. www.nytimes.com.

Pew Research Center, "Americans and 'Cancel Culture': Where Some See Calls for Accountability, Others See Censorship, Punishment," May 19, 2021. www.pewresearch.org.

Geoffrey R. Stone, "Sexual Expression and Free Speech: How Our Values Have (D)evolved," American Bar Association, 2023. www.americanbar.org.

United States Courts, "What Does Free Speech Mean?" www.uscourts.gov.

Rebeka Zeljko, "Debate over Free Speech Versus Hate Speech on College Campuses Raises Censorship Concerns," *California Aggie* (Davis, CA), January 19, 2023. www.theaggie.org.

INDEX